Migrating Minds

A Collection of Poetry and Prose

D1550228

Migrating Minds
First Published in 2004 by
MS Publications
Mid-Sutton Community Centre
Dublin 13.
ISBN No 0 – 9548438

Copyright© Individual Authors 2004
Special Thanks to Paula Meehan, Pat Boran,
and Theo Dorgan for their valuable contribution.

Paula Meehan- Sea poems. Previously published
in *Metre,* a literary journal.

The Publisher acknowledges financial
assistance from Fingal County Council

Fingal County Council
Comhairle Contae Fhine Gall

Cover photo courtesy of Brent Nicastro
Set in Type Baskerville
Design and layout by Conor O' Malley

Printed by **ColourBooks Ltd**. Baldoyle Industrial Estate, Dublin 13.

Contents   *Migrating Minds*

Introduction

To be asked by fellow writers to pen an introduction to this locally produced book at this hour of my life is a great honour for me. Our hope in compiling this book is that the folklore and stories we have penned will enrich people. The adventures of Saints, Sailors, Smugglers and Rogues or indeed any of the contributions, may be used as a resource to trigger the imagination of children of all ages.

When reading this book I would suggest that you look for our themes of coming and going, loss and identity, themes of living in the world, settling down, which may be of itself a counter theme to migration.

Following the success of his book the "The poet asks why" Tommy Delaney suggested last Christmas that we produce a book by ourselves. I hope you find our efforts are worth the cover price and that your praise and criticism will help us to reflect the creative experience. It was especially heartening to find such willingness amongst well known writers, Paula Meehan, Pat Boran, Theo Dorgan, to share their refined feelings with us.

It would be churlish of me to single out any individual. Suffice to say it was an enlightening experience and a privilege to work together. In this book there are a mixture of country people, local Dubs and also those who came from far off lands. This mixture of people from all areas makes a wonderful mix of style and variation, which I hope you will enjoy.

John O Malley

Brent Geese
John Walsh

Breasting   To fatten

    across the   their feathered

        wintery   fuselage   And praising

          morning   and cackle   the great

            sky   gossip   northern

            lines of   as they graze.   Skies that stretch

            Brent   Talking of   all day

      geese whir   the long flight   into long

    their way   northwards to   silver midnight.

  to other   the grassy fields

pastures.   Of Greenland.

If I Deny Seawrack
Máiride Woods

It's not that I don't remember, Daddy,
The fat veronica hedges on Dalriada,
Garron's wise profile, those Scottish lighthouses
Or the circle of men by the curfew tower.
Together we searched Glenann for Oisin's grave
Though your stories were of distant Kerry.

It's not that we even belonged here
Transplanted to an Antrim of clans
Where ours was the foreign surname.
Sucking my barley sugar I would mediate
The brightness of fuchsia and accent
While your eyes turned inwards to your Reeks.

It's not that I've forgotten the graveyard
Where your name has joined the neighbours in stone
Faraway lighthouses still cast their beams
Over the restless Moyle of my mind.
The places of childhood are like seawrack
Their smell sticks to you.

Paint Brushes (for Bayside school)
Sue Brown

Seventeen paint brushes lying quiet in a room
full of light and colour.
Egg cups, yoghurt cartons, shiny tops
and dull grey sinks
and the tent-like easels where young hearts camp
happy in the splashing. Quiet now.

I polish the table, just stroking
their extra strokes and splashes.
This is love - to touch, and let it pass.
To keep the room almost tidy, and ready

Red Furry-Coated Friend

I see you from the road at hilly Aughavannagh,
Spread-eagled in the near corner of the sloping green field,
Your head sideways tucked,
And swear you are just sleeping.

On this dusk dull December day,
The harsh winds contrast with your earth snuggle.
Two magpies and two hooded crows stand sentinel
On nearby giant granite boulders, black beaks blood smeared.

My heart denies what my mind knows.
The small stone I throw
Expects you to run
Swiftly to mother-waiting safe covert,

But moves you not,
Red furry-coated friend.
I climb the barbed wire fence,
To sense your life force,

Your soul reluctant to leave your still body
My kindred spirit, my madra ruadh.
Your peaceful face and sleeping eyes contradict
The grim messages written in some fleshless ribs.

I would take you with me
To evermore adorn my mantel
But you were too perfect
To be by man restored

Instead you will live in my memory
And in my soul possessed,
Together we will conspire to cheat death
And defy inflicted gunshot wounds of trigger-happy man.

With night's dark mantle about to fall
On your wind-swept frozen field-bed
I leave your full-furry-brush-body
To rest beneath the glitter of a million stars

I will always treasure your gift to me,
Rejoicing in life's full-glow sleeping,
Remembering the quiescence of life's journey's end,
Celebrating your personification in death.

John Haughton

Low Tide
Pat Boran

The tide goes out in the north bay
and the obsessive mapmaker god must be -
all those contours and coastlines, the courses of rivers -
starts over from scratch: filigree

of spume, broken zigzag of grass
and reed, the bulbous, morphing progress
of cloud formations…So much to be remade
and to be remade again. Nothing left

as it was even minutes ago. For each trickle
an original route to the sea; over each stone
or pebble, for each barely visible grain
of sand, and in each successive moment,

a new dome of light. And the reflection
of the clouds, masking and unmasking sky,
perfectly co-ordinated in each one of them…
An utterly incredible, pointless exercise

in which a father stands still a moment to watch
his son playing in the sand and instantly knows
that at some point in the future he would trade
his whole life for any one moment on this shore.

Cycle Off
John O' Malley

We gave the best bike to Kevin.
He used it up to the last day.
That Sunday he horsed
up and down the cycle-way.
Now looking down at The Nevada
his blue eyes said it all then.
Bewildered by what he saw,
no release from overloading.
Calm came, but not in a permanent
easy way for the rest of us
left behind.

Smoked Out
Thomas Delaney

Outside they sit and stand, cigarette in hand
Like lost aliens in a foreign land.
They need the fag, O boy do they need that drag
They have been evicted and restricted
They need that smoke, while disregarding that stroke.

They are viewed with amusement and bemusement
They sit in the wind, sometimes without a friend
Adorned with coats and gloves they huddle like doves.
Hats and scarves are worn, by that thoughtless wind they are
blown.

We are different they feel, we will definitely not kneel
We are entitled to puff, and be in a huff.
We blow smoke, but not at folk
We are a match for anyone on our patch.

We light up to be blown out, without doubt
Discomfort is now our blaring trumpet
We feel that the minister was very sinister
We are now left out in the cold, with thoughts so very bold.

5 - 4 -2004

Whoof
Paddy Glavin

There's a slate loose on my roof
Storms are not the only cause,
I pray that we are weatherproof.

For the moment there's no reproof
And we can afford a pause,
It's only a slate loose on the roof.

We're in the kitchen sitting aloof
Sipping whiskey, ignoring laws
Hoping we are foolproof.

Every house has faults: that's no spoof
And we accept the flaws,
But there's a slate loose on my roof.

From the black hole we hear a woof
Oh, we must not lose our equipoise.
Though I hope we are weatherproof.

The landlord arrived on the hoof
Ranting on about a clause,
It's only a slate loose on the roof
I hope we are weatherproof.

Smugglers, Saints, Sailors, and Rogues
Sue Brown

I live in 16 Sutton Downs, and look out from the window of a modern semi-detached home on a landscape that was boggy marsh inhabited by geese and wild fowl fifty years ago. In autumn, migrating geese still waddle near the train station in the mornings, on Sutton Court field or the nearby strand in the afternoon, and then fly to bed down on Bull Island at night. Such a landscape might seem unlikely to have earlier marks of man, but it does. For if you follow the old right of way which runs behind Sutton Downs, you will come to the old churchyard.

The children are sure it is haunted by the ghosts of sea mariners washed up, and buried there. They tell stories of smugglers, and truly the north coast of Dublin Bay is pockmarked by smugglers' caves. In bad storms the sea washes over the wall that protects the Dublin– Howth road, lapping at the foot of the cemetery's hill. Solemnly, children have warned me 'the mad nun' walks there, and brings accidents. Yet the church itself rests on peaceful ground locals believe had been a holy Celtic site even before St. Berreck parted from St. Kevin at Glendalough to set up a beehive hut here and watch over the water. The green and sunny peace of Glendalough seems to have spread here, where land touches the Irish sea, and wild wading birds feel safe. By moonlight the simple grey stone chapel looks as natural as rock hummocked out of the ground. Men built here, but the birds have lived here longer and roost here still.

The chapel, once referred to as Kill-beragh (Killbarrack) is indeed probably connected with St. Berreck (or Barroc), who left Monaghan to study under St. Kevin. When he had crossed the

Boyne and was passing through Bregia, he strewed a trail of mir acles, and the Regulus of the district gave him a place in his territory, first called Dysert-Beraigh or Berack, and later Killberagh, or Kilbarrack. In later years, but before the Norman invasion of 1169, a stone church was dedicated here, which was re-edified in the 15th century and is the existing ruin. Sailors indeed have been buried here. Another source refers to the chapel being dedicated to Mary, Star of the Sea, in the 14th century, and prayer being offered there for sailors and passengers lost in shipwrecks after wild storms.

The Martyrology of Donegal also calls this place Cill-Mona (church on marshy land) and mentions that Polan of Killmona (Paul, Paulinus) is perhaps Paul, master of St. David of Wales. He belonged to the Community of St. Fiac and was a missionary to the Isle of Man with St. German, the island's first bishop. According to The Short History of Dublin Parishes, 'his name still survives in "Stapolan" a townland near Baldoyle'.

Not far away is the little church of St. Fintan, a church patchily rebuilt down the centuries. The ruins include a belfry from the 13th century, and earlier work dating back to the 9th century, probably built on the site of a 7th century oratory. The St. Fintan giving it its name may be a Fintan who befriended the monk St. Comgall of Clontarf; he was possibly sent for missionary work in the Howth area, where Christianity took root as early as the 6th century.

Nearer Howth harbour lies Ireland's Eye island called Edria by Richard of Cirencester, and termed Irland by marauding Danes who added a suffix 'ei' meaning island. Toward the end of the 7th century three sons of Nessan- Dichull, Manissa, and Nelug-retreated here to build a house of prayer. This was first ravaged in 702 by sea pirates from the English coast. It was later rebuilt in stone (c.900 AD) and survived to be subsequently plundered by Danes. The present ruin is 10th or 11th century, with a vaulted chancel and a roundheaded western doorway, and the remnant foundations of a round tower. It was a little church much used till the 13th century when St Mary's, Howth became the centre of the area's church life. When its life was flourishing there from about the 7th century, a beautiful copy of the four gospels was made on the island. It is called The Garland of Howth and is kept safe in Trinity College's manuscript collection.

But Howth has a much longer history than nine centuries back. Shoredwellers lived in the area from about 3,500 BC hunting woodland red deer, hare and pig, and catching fish. Even then faithful dogs helped out, and the old footpath that skirts the western wall of Howth demense was trod by many feet and paws. It may have connected to the path at the foot of my garden. East of the demesne it still runs through the grounds of the Dominican Convent of Santa Sabina along the south shore of Howth Head, following what was then the coast. For as the Ice Age ended, seas rose and the Atlantic surged over the isthmus, turning Howth into an island. Here, Professor Frank Mitchell excavated a kitchen midden he dates from 3875 BC. He thinks that a group called the Larnian Folk had migrated to Dublin Bay. A later trace (c 2500 BC) left by Stone Age people is the dolmen (portal grave) in Howth demense. An early legend called this Finn's Quoit, which the giant had thrown from the Bog of Allen. A later one termed it Aideen's grave, Aideen having died of love and grief after the death of her heroic spouse Oscar, at the Battle of Garva near Tara in 284 AD. Certainly many stories of Finn associate him with this area. He and his men are said to have trained in the for est here, and Finn once received a visit from a mysterious lady love, the White Lady, when she sailed into Howth harbour. Later, Diarmuid and Grainne hid from Finn in its caves. So the children are right to imagine they can stride on the same land as the Fianna did, and to picture his young warriors and their beautiful horses in full flight over the hill of Howth, hooves pounding like the pounding sea.

Since that time there has been a light set on the hill to keep ships from crashing on the rocks. Ghosts of lost mariners haunt this coast, for each generation has seen terrible wrecks, and valiant human efforts to warn, and to save survivors.

The coast has also survived invasion. Vikings sailed here, coming as raiders, and then settling. Abutting Sutton Park is the Baldoyle Road and its strand. Baldoyle is connected with the Danish invasion of 852 which plundered an earlier colony of Fionn Gaill (white strangers: Norwegians). The Danes valued the estuary as a safe haven for longboats, and the land was renamed Baile Dubhgail (town of dark strangers). These different Vikings opposed each other in the melee of the Battle of Clontarf. In Howth village St. Mary's, commonly called the Abbey, was founded by Sitric, Danish king of Dublin in 1052. He erected part of the structure, which was added to in the 13th century, and in 1430 Christopher, 13th Baron of Howth, added to it and gave a three-light window. The tomb has figures of him and his wife Elizabeth. Not an abbey at all, but a prebend (church dependent on a greater cathedral) this became the medieval focus of the church in this area. But at this time our local chapel was also flourishing.

None of this lore is forgotten in the area. Local schools keep alive the names of Fintan and Nessan (who by all accounts was not a saint but fathered three holy sons!) The cemetery of the chapel is still in use. Its most famous burial is an ungodly one, the 'sham squire' Francis Higgins (his gravestone long since wrecked) who betrayed Lord Edward Fitzgerald to arrest and death. Higgins' colourful life, rising from 'a bare-legged boy carrying pewter quarts in Fishamble St.' to convict, swindler, 'sham squire' and justice of the peace, informer and ruthless government spy, is detailed in W.J. Fitzpatrick's book The Sham Squire. On his tombstone he begged forgiveness—and still, the land receives the good and the bad, accepts all, and offers to all the hope of a good life.

Many thanks to Dr. Vincent McBrierty for his substantial help in preparing this piece. He is the editor of *The Howth Peninsula: Its History, Lore and Legend*, available in Howth library. Thanks also to Mr. Paddy Glavin who gave valuable suggestions. The idea first came from listening to local children, and I hope its outcome will be more tales for them to share with us.

TRIBUTE TO A TRIBUTARY
Eddie Phillips

This river of my childhood had no name.
Running alongside our garden, lying into the bank: a child getting a love.
It went under the bridge conversing, like friends leaving after a visit,
Adding more water from the Wicklow hills to the Slaney River.
At first convergence a last gift to small boys: a corner cavity under the bank;
Raftered with tall-tree roots; furnished with washed rocks.

A half mile back the drama took place.
With a salmon's urgency a fat deep gush extruded through the narrow sluice,
Flooding the watercourse that lazed its shored-up way,
To fill the miller's pond to its overflow and thunderous waterfall,
Leaving the main congregation to assist in the baptism of the great wheel.
Water returning by two routes to its river, continuing,
To many similar casual encounters.

The great wheel, cast-iron, buckets of oaken timbers,
Rising out of the deep sump, white water still running off,
With poised pond meting out roaring replenishment,
To outweigh resistance from cog-wheeled shaft within,
It drove millstones, sack hoist, grain screener, oat roller, grinder, and generator:
The cogs of first transmission worn to chisel edges.

This river, like the angel who tells nothing about herself,
Eternally humble and therefore ignored seemed unwanted unloved.
I thought once to enquire its name but lost interest.
Yet in its casual passing-by it gave the miller and family a living.
It was the Rio Grande to a seven year-old cowboy.
It is the presence of a soul departed to this migrant.

Leap of faith
Máiride Woods

You stand in a green and pleasant meadow,
A low fence enclosing your leafless form,
Ropes holding you. Can dead trees escape?
Or resurrect? Farmer covering himself, I think
As down the motorway I whizz,
A metal-shelled hermit,
Listening for breath from a dying love affair:
He doesn't call.

You hold out your blackened branches
Soliciting pity or whatever. I'm glad
They bury people quickly. Cover over
My gnarled and disillusioned limbs
With dockets, lists and till-receipts….
Yet driving homewards with the stars
I glimpse you skeletal and ghostly
Keeping watch with your comrades.

I imagine you breaking out,
Cutting the ropes
Leaping over that incongruous fence,
Over the motorway, over the seasons
Reaching the rolling parklands of the soul
Where you scatter your shining leaves
With joyous bounty.

Wrighting
John Walsh

Finding the material is painful.
Most of it has been cast aside.
Getting the block with a true grain
In the charnel yard of the mind
Takes patience and cunning.

The early hacking is pleasing.
Cold-chiselling the rough stuff
And letting the spalls dance and fly.
Then finding the inner shape.
This is true creation.

Now we know the answer;
Is there something there?
Next will come the finishing,
The rebuilding and the polishing.
And knowing when to stop.

To find that stage of fittingness
Where all the words are tight.
If we could fashion one poem a year
A lifetime might produce
A slim collection.

First Intended Words
Eddie Phillips

With a genuflection to THE Word

I returned a book to Sheila,
Aptly enough an angel,
Apt the title, *Words From God*,
Aptly further, not my book.
But where His words exposed me,
A line I carry and use
Was written down
In the margin in rubbable pencil.
With eraser poised I asked myself,
Why not publish to a readership of one?
It stayed.

The line: O Lord to play my part,
        Please lead me back to an innocent heart.

Apart from the folded poem I hid
In a coat on a cloakroom hook,
- My God what an innocent heart -
To Dorothy the Girl in the Red Tartan Skirt,
I had no desire to write for other eyes.

Soundings
Paddy Glavin

Conor's recital was a tribute
to an out-of-tune piano.
A prelude in moonlight
on the lawn of a house

renowned for hospitality.
Neighbours and friends
toasted the instrument
on its way to the skip,

easing the surrender
of abandoned things
before a slayer
sundered the ivory keys.

The heartstrings lay bare on the grass
though the soundboard is intact.

In a schoolroom a teacher
uncovered a piano
and crossed bridges of scales
to a suite of melodies.

Her hands floated lightly
on the keyboard.
Little clusters of notes
gave a melancholy feeling

a Haiku for the piano?

For her we clapped out
the syllables of our names
and sang from the heart

The heartstrings lay bare on the grass
though the soundboard is intact.

CHRISTMAS
John Haughton

Crowded street
Freezing sleet
Robin in the snow

Holly boughs
Warm fires glow
Welcoming

Childhood toys
From Santa Claus
Adults remembering

Christ Child
Manger-tied in
Swaddling clothes

Reindeer
Good cheer
No fear

Angel sings
Hope springs

ETERNAL

APPLE TIME
John O' Malley

The world is after orchard, orchard
That spells fortune.
Over a wall though there is a mortal fall.

We would prepare the ships
Gleaming oh so small.

The eyes of a dove are sure
Let them last-wooer, overall.

You spoke of the armour,
Hitherto with provision we set sail.

Our men will lie down,
The breeze carries a great deal.

Remember the winter alone,
The seal has to be torn.

Come wonder chartered,
Allow the new meal,

And tender hearted
The talk is of here.

Commuting by Train
John Walsh

With sureness and a sense of ownership,
We occupy our seats by habit.
Nonchalantly reading our
Novels or papers.
Ignoring the well-kept gardens
Flitting by.
Uninterested in the plane
Dipping slowly towards the airport.
Unaware of our fellow travellers.
But the unfamiliar alerts us.
We sense the tension of the stranger.
The study of station names
By anxious tourists.
The inability of the visitor
To relax and let
The journey run its course
On predestined lines.
We take all this for granted,
Hiding our fragility in habit.
Commuting our lives away.

Down Our Street
Sue Brown

The blue twilight breathed quiet
full of life and then-extra-
across the night air rippled
the music of the violin
in the breeze. I was walking
down the road for a message.
I had been awhile alone,
and so was the player.
But his thoughts were shared
in the gentle pleading
in the half-light,
music threading the wind.

The Hill Trams
Paddy Glavin

The recent return of the trams to Dublin re-awakened memories in Stephen Byrne. His grandfather John loved history and told him of Dublin's old transport system. Trams left Nelson's Pillar for Blackrock, Kingstown and Dalkey, Clonskea, Rathgar and Terenure, Palmerstown Park, Rathmines, Ringsend and Sandymount and from the other side of the Pillar trams served Dollymount and Howth.

His granddad recalled a day when he and his classmates were at the edge of a schoolyard near Fairview when a strange parade appeared. They climbed the railings for a better view of a procession. Twelve new tramcars were on low-loaders drawn by several powerful horses. They were large open top vehicles gleaming in colours of marine blue and ivory white. The boys stood silently watching, ignoring the end of the break bell as the procession passed. At that moment John vowed to become a motorman on the trams.

He left school at fourteen and haunted the tram depot at Baldoyle. He inveigled permission to travel on the trams. With a hint of nostalgia in his voice he described his first journey on the open topped "Hill Tram". The vehicles passed over tracks inlaid on cobblestones through Sutton Cross from Sutton railway station, with bells ringing as it moved onto Strand Road. Originally this causeway was built on the seabed when Howth Head was an island. The tram powered from overhead cables travelled uphill now, on by St. Fintan's cemetery with Shielmartin hill on the left.

On the upper deck the morning sun reflected light from gorse and perfumed the air. On the lower deck the motorman varied the notches, skillfully negotiating the twists and turns. Around every bend John absorbed the breathtaking scenery. The bell clanged counter pointing the cry of a kittiwake. The tram became a magic carpet floating in an ever-changing landscape of hills, sea and sky. From "The Green" he saw the Bailey Lighthouse built on the narrow neck of a promontory. John discovered later this edifice was erected on a Fort of the last Milisian King of all Ireland. Perched now on the swaying tram, the view southwards across Dublin Bay with a backdrop of the mountains took his breath away.

At the summit, the main stop, the conductor Michael disappeared. The motorman Tom chatted to John telling him of the forthcoming descent when the tram would freewheel down the gradient to Howth station. He mentioned the view of Ireland's Eye, Lambay Island and much further north the Mountains of Mourne. He spoke of the legends of Howth Castle where in the "Mermaid's Tower" a female ghost visits at Easter and Christmas. She was a daughter of O'Byrne of Wicklow and was betrayed by a son of Lord Howth's.

John was even more fascinated when he heard the tale of Grace O' Malley. By custom the gates were closed at dinnertime, as was the practice when Grace called. She was slighted and kidnapped a son of Lord Howth's. He was returned provided that a place would be set for an unexpected guest, a tradition that is still maintained by the St. Lawrence family resident in the castle from the 13th century.

The conductor Michael returned, his face flushed. He stared at John saying

"So you want to be a tram man"?

John sensed the conductor's resentment and looked at Tom. The motorman's blue eyes twinkled as he spoke to Michael.

"Remember your own youth 'Me Aul Flower' and the bottles of whiskey
Mr. Jameson gives you".
The conductor snorted and replied.
"Does he know of the long hours we work from dawn 'till midnight"?

On the journey downhill Michael whined about the constant clanging of wheels, and the frost on his ears when he had to change trolleys in winter. John looked over beyond the harbour. He escaped again on a magic carpet gliding down through moraines and cairns where kings were buried. He glimpsed the colour of rhododendrons through trees on the St. Lawrence castle grounds.

By the time the tram was at Howth railway station, John felt as if he had descended from a higher place. He will bring his girl along next Sunday. He forgot about the complaining conductor, and wasn't discouraged and he later became a motorman, living his dream every day on the "Hill Trams".

The closure of the line in May 1959 heralded many changes in transport systems, but the wheel turned full circle when John's grandson became a driver on the Luas tram.

A Piece of Joinery
Eddie Phillips

I must have quiet and solitude there
In the assembling of your bookcase.
It is deliberate like gestation
Or even more
Intense like its prerequisite.

You've made a virgin space.
I will groom it with a slow amalgam of pieces
And I will leave to you
Honeyed virgin spaces.

Then you will want quiet and solitude there
For the assemblage, your books.

Whisking the Images
Máiride Woods

Discarded images; those gutted mussel-shells
That teeter so ungainly on the plates
After the guests have gone. *Is that all there is?*
I'm standing tired and soulful at my sink
Replaying the evening à la Peggy Lee:
A downbeat feast, the setting modest
The main dish tasty, friends relaxed and chirpy,
But did a kindred spirit speak or sing?

My Muse wears glasses like Darina Allen
She says my hand's too heavy with the flavourings
She advocates nouvelle cuisine: the poem pared
And glistening on its bed of meaning. But what is life
Without a flash of flambé? I'm whisking crazy images
To match the reds and yellows of that flouncy trifle
My mother used to make.

My Garden
John Haughton

My Garden
In Bloom
In June
And I
With Nature
In Tune

Forever and Ever
John O' Malley

School bends our fervent thought
Bring us back to rule.
Spare events that cost us naught
We needs must choose less destiny.

Make us wear our coat out.
Rain, effortless, easy pales
By September green over all
Then carve out these good.

You designate kind beholder
Theme arrogant, skilled ruler,
Back by our lies hidden
And forgive and teach us
Not to grow, grow- you know.
Why the morning worked wonders
Calling out and we came...

Evening went missed
By our sighs we were foxed.
Up on to the hill
Who comes back by way
Of that grin salvages
All of our excellence.

Though we are mild
Child our care innocent
Shames more to be good.
Yet beware of her somehow
Though she not be cold.
Mustn't she grow old
Whether by sand or rock
Give her deserving smiles
And that will not end,
I must not end.

Piseoga
John Walsh

My Grandmother lived in her parents' time.
Wrapped in the fear of eggs in the garden,
The evil eye on a calf
Or the changeling child.

The signs were well known;
Birds whistling after dark,
A black cat on the road,
A red-haired woman at dawn
Or a pair of magpies.

Falling cutlery foretold the visitor
And straw from the Christmas crib
Kept money in the purse.
A silver blessing in the hand of a child
And curing a sty with a golden ring.

Before her neighbours died
She heard the ban-shee cry.
The obligations were stronger
In the corpse house;
Stopping the clock,
Turning the mirror
And telling the hens.

May Day potions were collected
And all Saints Night observed.
Never refuse well water, she said.
It would bring bad luck.
And never enter a ring fort;
An injury sustained
Would see you to the grave.

Such were the customs
That kept her life in check.
Luck and misery were twin cats
Always sitting at her gate.

For My Father
Sue Brown

He played music full of anguish and question
but its beauty stilled the night air
to a deep twilight blue.
A cool wind rippled the strings
as his busy fingers plied
the human trades of living through working.

The quiet moonlight bathed the street;
each cobble's dark hump told a hundred stories
of walking men and women.
Beneath the stones the ground
crumbled, and cold, all earth was
waiting. But 'wait with a warm heart'
plays the music. To suffer is love.
And the stirred air, poor living struggling man, gently
tosses your garments. In the moonlit street,
waiting for daylight, thread colour aplenty
of heart's life, and loved in and by
the mystery, for each one and for all, play.

Send out blue notes like birds to heaven's summer
from the chilly landscape.
Message-carriers, grey-winged till they soar
over fields of warm wet light
and soften to a dusky white as they land.
Still the low honking to each other,
still the receiving by the Lord's cupped hand.
And His gentle eyes receiving questions.

And we just pale white birds in a blue-brightening sky.
Soft grey-barked, mossy green
trees of peace grow sweet and strong,
and angels hover over grass–beings
for whom to think is simply to sing,
so sweet the order of their days,
so full of love their glances at earth's pain.

Play through the night some remembered echo
tumbling to us (rolled by angels?)
from those skies, let the two
songs touch, and play oh play.

The Silver Lining
John Haughton

It was a bright morning at the end of June 1935. The sun was on its climb through the skies at the early hour of five and came streaming into Lady Heath's bedroom. The dazzling brightness of the morning and the dawn chorus of the birds could not be resisted. The symphony of birdsong was deafening and demanded attention. Lady Heath was not angry at the feathered winged wonders of the sky. She felt a strong affinity towards them, the masters of flight. She was their understudy. Human engineers could not match their gift of flight with all its intricacies. It would be a nice morning she thought to savor the ambience of the little idyllic village of Finglas and the surrounding area. Finglas and its quaint beauty held a special fascination for her. Having leisurely strolled through the countryside she would take her silver bird, the 'Silver Lining'. to flights real and fancy over the Royal Kingdom of Meath.

Her husband Jack was one with her in her morning plan and they both hurried themselves so that they would arrive at Finglas Bridge by taxi at the early hour of six o'clock. A narrow bridge spanned the River Tolka. Its setting was a thing of real beauty, unspoiled, romantic and serene. They would like to have lingered there, but they must slowly wend their way to another wonder, an oasis of flying machines in the fertile lands of Finglas. Kildonan Aerodrome was their destination.

Immediately north of Finglas Village was Ashgrove House and the welcome site of Parkes' Garage, with its immaculate chauffeurs and shining black taxis. They would avail of the services of one of these to complete the last leg of their journey to the aerodrome.

When they reached Kildonan, they alighted from the taxi and proceeded to the hangar. As they approached it, their steps quickened, imperceptibly, but steadily. Lady heath felt her heart beat quicker as she was irresistibly drawn to her plane, the Silver Lining. Home was where the hangar was and the hangar was at Kildonan, Finglas. The real feeling of home could be found in the whine of an aircraft engine, the smell of burnt fuel, the camaraderie of flying friends. Her special home was in the sky. Today, she had only one ambition, to fly the Silver Lining. Hugh Cahill had chosen the perfect place for an aerodrome.

She breathed the pure air deep into her lungs. It was so good to be alive. It was a flyer's day. She felt the green grass under her shoes, a sweet sensation. The open hangar stared out on the airfield, on the surrounding plains and on a vast expanse of sky devoid of any cloud. They pushed the Silver Lining out of the hangar area and with one turn of the propeller, Lady Heath spun the engine into life. She allowed the aircraft ample time for the engine to warm up. When Jack Williams removed the chocks from the wheels it was a clear signal for Lady Heath to begin her take off. The little craft began slowly, and then gathered speed as it raced along the smooth green carpet that was Kildonan. Having attained take-off speed the wheels parted company with the earth. The engine cowling rose smoothly up towards the horizon, pointing at the single cirrus-streaked sky. For a few moments she stared fixedly at the blue sky beyond the pitched up nose and the invisible propeller. The wings cut through the deep blue sward of the sky. Now and then she strained her eyes, searching meticulously into the dazzling brightness of the sun, for any aircraft that might be concealed within its glare. She could feel the unique uplifting feeling, that magical sensation all over, like a gull savoring the soft summer eddies along the cliff edge. She loved the free fresh wind in her face. It was as if the soaring wings of the little craft had suddenly filled with air, like the sails of a ship. Lady Heath craned her neck over the side of the cockpit and watched the grassy take-off ground of the airfield sliding back towards the leading edge of the left lower wing. The far boundary of the airfield slowly disappeared under the wing. It seemed as if by rising in the air, she had suddenly become a god, shaking off the human chrysalis. Lady Heath, as usual, had made the perfect take-off. She searched the sky for other aircraft but there were none to be seen. Her little craft had been absorbed into the friendly sky. The world aloft was pure brilliance. Her soft-featured face and pale blue wide-pupil eyes, behind wizard goggles, were absolutely still, lost in total concentration. Visibility was brittle-sharp and unlimited, while the sound of the engine filled the blue domed sky. Her ears were finely tuned to the music of the wires as her steady speed held a single prolonged note on the continuum of sound. She felt secure and content in the great aloneness, cushioned from reality, in the ambience of the Eternal.

["The Silver Lining", ISBN 0-9518504-2-3 {Ch. 18, p. 243ff,}]

An Angel Appears
Eddie Phillips

An angel appears inside my space at my shoulder,
Which places me within the span of her wings,
Accepted and welcomed.

Just once under her wing of Dove-white, then
Beholding randomly in my vision:
Beholding eyes that pour Peace into the heart;
Beholding eyes with messages for a legion soul.

An angel appears and tells not one thing about herself.
Eternally humble. I could keep company with her forever.

The Ghost Bus
Paddy Glavin

Tram-bells echoed
outside the GPO, a temple
summoning the protesters
to march into the sixties.

I had walked before at Pentecost
and on route marches over hills.
I used to tramp, tramp miles
of dream-roads to meet my father

on his way home at weekends.
Then he would carry me on the crossbar
and cycle between hedgerows,
a guard of honour all the way to Listowel.

But now it was midnight on May-Eve
The starlings' roosts disturbed
by raised voices
and the footfall stamp of protest.

We had no banners on display
But anger showed on our faces.
Someone played a harmonica
along The Appian Way.

While pedestrians laughed
Larkin hands in the sky
ignited fire in the marchers' eyes
though they could not see the stars

dimmed by the glare of neon.
A leopard stalked in their minds
and melted the amphaloi
of the legion that night.

I'm offering this sequence of 5 sonnets called **Sea** set on the estuary and up Burrow Beach. They were previously published in *Metre*, a literary journal.

Paula Meehan
For Tony Walsh

I

From Scratch   by Paula Meehan

To begin again: my hands sifting sand
at the sea's edge, and nothing to be done.
All day to do it in. To start again
from scratch; a driftwood stick, a hazel wand
to scribe your name deep in the newfound land
the ebbing tide has granted me. The sun
is a time bomb tossed to the blue heaven;
clouds shadow my script, shadow my young hand.
A heron takes flight as if not knowing
yet what its own wings can do. There are reams
of Brent geese landing with their hungry song.
At the tide's edge your name — going, going
gone with the turning tide. What was mere dream
of empire — dissolved, wrecked, gone badly wrong.

II

High Tide by Paula Meehan

When we stole out of the sleeping estate
down to the sea shore, we were thieves of night.
We were thieves of grief, we were thieves of light.
Hand in hand, each the other's chosen mate.

We wanted to copperfasten our fate
in the sound of, in the face of, in sight
of, the highest tide either one of us might
know. We wanted to feel that mortal weight.

The neighbours must have shifted in their dreams
and turned, or sighed, or called out of their sleep
some lost love's name, some unmourned daughter's death;
as in: my Sarah, my Nancy, my Liam.
Lyric of their secret fret the sea keeps —
the drowned forever singing their last breath.

III

Bounden   by Paula Meehan

I have to go down to the sea again.
I cannot resist the pull. The full moon
is drawing me back: the ebbtide a tune
of retreat. I surrender. All that remains
of my life I offer. My animal pain.
Poetry — you can keep it. It's been my ruin.
For so many years I was gifted; boon
presents now as burden, as curse, as bane.

The islands appear, they vanish, return.
A dog worries her image in a pool;
disturbs the mirror, digs deep in the sand,
self unfathomable. And I, who learn
this craft at the expense of art: mere fool
that the sea abandons high on dry land.

IV

Handsel by Paula Meehan

I take my black dog down to the winter sea;
a mere drop in the ocean each salt tear.
The north wind is bitter, threatening snow;
it whips up the waves, it whines through the dunes.
A small boat is wrecked on the rocks — dragged free
of its mooring, dismasted, all its gear
and tackle cast on the tide. A lone crow
blown from the woods pecks at a sliced pan strewn
on the water.   O the sea neither gives
nor takes as we fancy. The sea has no needs,
nor worries, nor wants. If we call it 'she' —
an ur mother — it is because salt lives
in our blood. And grief drops salt like seeds;
brings home shells in pockets — memory.

V

Ashes by Paula Meehan

The tide comes in; the tide goes out again
washing the beach clear of what the storm
dumped. Where there were rocks, today there is sand;
where sand yesterday, now uncovered rocks.

So I think on where her mortal remains
might reach landfall in their transmuted forms,
a year now since I cast them from my hand
— wanting to stop the inexorable clock.

She who died by her own hand cannot know
the simple love I have for what she left
behind. I could not save her. I could not
even try. I watch the way the wind blows
life into slack sail: the stress of warp against weft
lifts the stalling craft, pushes it on out.

Geisha Lives
Máiride Woods

The geisha cherries are dancing in rows
Tossing their curls in lacy ringlets
Between the geometric lake and the Science block.
Gifts between great ones, arranged
For others' pleasure, they turn
The frothy underskirts of Tokyo springs
To Belfield's muddy skies, stillness
The pearly pistil in their carefree dance.

I imagine being born to geishahood…

Body over mind, that ghost-life of the senses,
Blossoms beyond any clichéd Japan
Of inscrutable satin and embroidered fans. Among
Those marionettes my clumsiness vanishes. I trade
My voice for daggered stillness, for forms
I don't believe in. Within my gnarled heart
Lie all the lopped-off routes I could have taken
-Anchorite and geisha, empress and slave.

A Prayer: A Seed, A Cloud
Eddie Phillips

10pm 31st December 2000

A prayer incensed: a fistful of seed,
Stars on black, fertile awareness.

Unwhispered, formed in thought.

Fine sand for throwing into the eyes
Of a close familiar enthusing the finer points
Of a favourite sin.

Creamery Boy 1959
John Walsh

This slow death on the road to the creamery;
It turns my heart to clay.
With tankards of warm milk behind me
And the horse's head nodding away.

My brother emigrated to Coventry
He'll come home next Christmas I'm sure
With a fifty pounds in his pocket
That'll cover both drink and the cure.

My fingers are sore from the milking.
My hair's turning grey at the ears.
My clothes and my boots are past mending
And my soul is rotting with fears.

Should I leave this prison called farming?
And turn my back on this land?
While the spirit is still within me
And some strength is left in my hand?

Tomorrow I would tender my notice
And buy a boat-ticket to Crewe.
But the fears of a lifetime restrict me
And melt my hopes like the dew.

The Road To Autumn
Theo Dorgan

The wind swings in from the pale north
Over dry land drenched in the smell of the sea,
And the old men shuffle anxiously
From one patch of sunlight to the next.

The swallows are gone now, a week since.
The school door is battered from the inside
By voices of muted panic, a sudden tide -
The damned, condemned to perpetual life indoors.

The road to autumn opens through the wood
That is itself opening quietly to the sky.
Where once was solid wall, now the quick eye
Pierces through to the low smudge of the west

And every eye in town is drawn away
To the brown leaves and the yellow leaves and the red,
Skirling & stopping then drifting out ahead
On the road to autumn, where every heart is bare.

For Gabriel Fitzmaurice

Rapture
John O' Malley

Everlastingly sing
With a lyrical murmur,
Later our voices
Reach ecstasy.
The value of stillness
Gazing at the needs
Of learned love,
Dictating at evening time
Until work is done.
Fair picture of evening
Rarely captured
Basking in repose.
Charm us with an endeavour
Gathered from afar.

Raindrops on the window

Sue Brown

Like silver worm trails
of invisible creatures
they wind down into grey shadows
of the white windows edges.
Do they slip shape there
become something else?
Is it magic? Moonlight snails?
And why, sometimes
when I light a lamp
are there beatings at the windows
showers of melting stars
tapping to come in?

Memories of a Country Childhood
Frances Glavin

Looking back, it seems that it was always summer. Oh yes, I have recollections of building snowmen and feeding starving robins but my main recollection is of one sunny day following another. There seemed to be endless things to do. We lived on a farm, so we woke to the sound of hens cackling, cows lowing and the swish of swallows' wings as they sped unerringly into their nests- in the barn.

One of our favourite pastimes was looking for birds'nests. I have a very vivid memory of the day I found my first one. I had been envious of my brothers and sisters who kept count of every nest they found while my tally was nil. One day I found my first nest at the top of the orchard. I was incoherent with excitement. I raced down the path shouting my news and it was some time before my family calmed me down enough to find out if my news was disastrous or triumphant!

My parents were teachers in the local primary school about two miles away. My older sister ran all the way to school lugging a brother with her. I was allowed to go to school with two older brothers. We never took the road. That would have been too dull. Instead, we went through the fields, exploring a different route every day. Of course, we were never on time but my eldest brother put the blame on my short four-year-old legs. One day we came to a stream. Paddy straddled the stream, gave me his coat to hold and started to lift me across. I thought it would help if I jumped into his arms. I ended up in the cold, clear water, drenching the coat and myself. The boys brought me down to school and Paddy went to my mother to explain the mishap. I don't know how he slid out of trouble. I suspect now that he blamed the whole incident on me because she was not angry but full of sympathy for her damp offspring. "Go on home with Paddy, alanna," she said, "and shure you needn't come back." My father, however, took me out of the boy's company and I had to join the morning sprint with my sister. It put me off jogging for life!

We were the owners of a vintage car, vintage even in those days. Every summer my parents got out their paintbrushes and did a thorough painting job on it in a revolting shade of yellow. They started one Friday morning and of course, it was not dry by evening when my father wanted to go into the local town to do the weekly shopping. He drove it around the field for about ten minutes. It dried all right, but he forgot about flies and midges. Not everyone can boast of a car with thousands of creepy crawlies embedded in the paintwork. The car was strictly for utility and never, in my memory, used for viewing the countryside on Sunday afternoons.

We had games for wet days and fine days. The latter were no problem. We played handball against the gable end of an out-house and when we tired of that we played what we called hand-ball with tennis racquets. The modern form is known as Squash! On wet days, one of our games was to hang a laundry bag stuffed with rags in a doorway. This improvised punch ball was great fun. The score was counted by the number of hits on the other person's head so we ducked, weaved and danced. Cassius Clay would have been envious of us.

My brother and myself invented a new game, which enthralled us throughout one summer. My father brought home an old roll book from the school so we decided to start a roll call for the hens. Firstly we had to name the hens and to learn to recognise them. This was surprisingly easy for two observant youngsters and we had great fun in identifying each by its comb, the shape of its tail or the infinite variety of shades on its wings or back. We must have been quite young at the time as the names were childish – Kingy, Queenie, Jelly, Cornflour and Scut-tail. The one bantam was called Fairy. We then started our roll book. We visited the hen house after each cackle of achievement and put a tick after the name of the hen which delivered an egg. In the evening the non-laying quota got a big fat nought! The man who took away the unproductive hens arrived in the autumn. Immediately my father called for the roll-book. We were amazed, as he had often said "Pschaw! Ye're only coddin' yereselves. Ye don't know one hen from the other." We were given the heady power of deciding which one went to the old hens' home. Fairy was exempt from banishment. Even though she laid only about four eggs in the year she was a pet and a kind of mascot. We didn't fret over the loss of the hens. We knew there was an end to living things – to cats, dogs, and farm livestock, and my mother would get a fresh clutch of chickens in the spring..

A neighbour called one day with a wriggling object in his coat pocket. It was a lively terrier pup with black and tan spots. He was promptly christened Ginger and from then on became part of our lives. He came everywhere with us and as he grew older we took him off to hunt for rabbits.We often arrived home in a jubilant mood with a fat rabbit for my mother to clean and cook. I'm sure she dreaded our hunting expeditions.

We stored potatoes in an outhouse and this inevitably drew rats. I hated and feared them even though I remember gazing at one in fascination as he wriggled out of the hen-house on his back, an egg tenderly clasped to his furry stomach. My father bought a cage for the rats and the first day after he baited it we raced to the storehouse and, sure enough, there was a rat in the cage running hither and thither, spitting in a frenzy. I kept my distance as I had been told that if I opened my mouth and happened to swallow a rat's spit I would die more or less on the spot. I didn't think this was true but I had no intention of putting the matter to the test! My father took the cage and Ginger into a field and released the rat. Ginger pounced but wasn't quick enough. The rat bit his nose and escaped. The next day we had a repeat performance. Ginger leaped, caught the rat by the back, shook hard, and it died instantly. He dispatched others in the same way.

I had no fear of heights in those days and often climbed the steep ladder to the hay piled nearly up to the roof of the barn. I was usually armed with a few apples and a book. Ginger wasn't pleased at being left out and howled furiously on the ground. One day I held his paws, put the front ones on the rung of the ladder, and then the back ones. Our clever dog got the message fairly quickly and soon was able to climb up, guarded anxiously by me in case he slipped. He lay contentedly beside me as I browsed through my book. When it came to coming down the ladder Ginger had to be carried as he refused point blank to go down backwards. That dog always had to see where he was going!

Calamity struck without warning. Ginger got sick and was unable to do more than give a feeble wag of his tail. He lay on a bed of hay in the cow-house warmed at night by the breath of the cows. My father diagnosed pneumonia and got some tablets and slid them down Ginger's throat. Anxiously we waited, and no patient had so many visitors. On Sunday morning we had our weekly big treat - a cooked breakfast. This particular Sunday my brother visited the patient before his meal and came back in high excitement. Ginger could lift his head. We ran out with our precious sausages and Ginger swallowed one or two. We knew then that he would live and he was his own self in a short time.

One of my saddest memories when I was away at school was getting the bad news in a letter from my mother that Ginger was dead. He had been missing for some days and eventually my father found him on a neighbour's lands. Other dogs had killed him. This was the part that hurt most. I didn't know that dogs do this sort of thing in a fight over a bitch, and I felt sick at heart over poor Ginger's fate. He will always hold a special place in my memory. He appears in most of the family photographs and even though we had other dogs before and after his reign, Ginger was special.

I was the youngest of six children and my closest companions were my two older brothers. It was a case of " If you can't fight 'em join 'em". Well I joined them and fought them as well! I could box as well as any boy until blows to the chest began to hurt quite a lot. Childhood was coming to an end but those enchanted years are a treasure stored in my memory bank, ready to be savoured in nostalgic moments.

WONDER WEBS OF FREEDOM
(A Poem to Chris Anyanwu in Gombe Prison)

In Gombe Prison Chris Anyanwu waits
Between noise and silent contemplation
Outside the World waits
To shine a Light of Freedom

Time and Tide wait
Starry Skies wait
Winter waits for spring
A Rose cries 'Freedom'

Ogoni People wait
To sing and dance dark clouds away
For Sunny Summer days
And Whisper 'Freedom'

Chris Anyanwu waits
While Pen-friends
Patiently, Spiderlike
Weave wonder webs of Freedom

John Haughton

Homeland
Paddy Glavin

On the lookout
I listen for a wing-beat;
halloo of Brent Geese
as they wheel from their flight path
onto glistening mudflats.
With flocks of migrants
they feed and bathe in sea pools
left by a flowing tide.
I moved from the southwest
making a landfall in fifty-four

moulting for years and flightless
until I grew new feathers
and landed near the lagoon by Dublin Bay.
Sometimes I hear spring singing on the estuary
in beak-blue mussel shells
where a breeze carries aromas
from the salt-marsh,
while shy flowers of asters
and sea-lavender emerge in morning sun
their leaves raised to the light.

Tiny ripples on a silt
surface from the underworld
home of sandworms and cockles.
The hungry waders
like gravediggers
know where to dip and dig.
A cormorant perched
on a discarded traffic cone
watches over flocks of birds
living without compromise.

Identical
Eddie Phillips

The mistake you make with me is:
You know you know me, so
You opine within earshot about
What meets the eye, the substance.
Without realising I'm a *Gemini*,
You talk about one twin
In the presence of the other.
You have to watch and listen for the teamwork.
Yes, we're a formidable team
Jem and I.

22nd Jan. 2003

Unwind
John O' Malley

We all long
For a genuine voice,
A slowing or swaying of pace.

Immaculate
Consider the grace
Perturbed.

At one with their rate,
Vague words overblown
I explode.

Sharply you reasoned me on,
No more than a sharing of taste
Boiled over
Mine, Yours?
Away from the chase.

Southern Words
John Walsh

It's all very well for Northern folk
To call a shovel a spade,
To sink the phrase to the hilt
And blind us with the Word
Between the eyes.
It's all very different down South.
Here we play with words.
We press them and test them
And let them be.
We know that the clarity
Is not as clear as it might seem.
It is a stone under water
Shining a refracted beauty,
But take it out and it is
Not perfect anymore.
Down South our language is a veil.
We do not know the answer.
Solutions lie elsewhere.
To us language is not a wedge
To split the true from false.
We use it to bandage feelings
And conceal the pain.
Yet if we are all to change
And learn to speak as one;
We need another tongue
Perhaps?

A Place for Pangur Bán
Máiride Woods

I was looking for an empty space
To plant a common or garden
Poem. No orchid, no special
Requirements of sun or shade. Any
Word-free ledge would suffice.

There is the back of the painting,
The artist's dreams undusted,
The margin beside the crossword, the circle
Behind the guitar strings
Awash with hidden music.

A slim and flexible verse
Could bed down in any corner
To wait on quickening. Who knows
The Spirit might descend
Even on a Pay-and-Display ticket.

Words blur, get orphaned
Of meaning like paper-boats;
Their chances of survival no wider than
The vellum margin where a monk wrote
Of his little white twelfth century cat.

Finding Anna Livia
Máiride Woods

The Dublin I came to know was the Dublin of the fifties, a ramshackle place overstocked with dilapidated churches and my parents' memories. It was my birthplace and true home, though I didn't actually live there. Circumstances - of the pecuniary kind so well-known to Mr. Joyce – kept us apart.

We were exiles with the exile's lop-sided view of the world. Home was best but which home? For most of the year I lived in a beautiful part of the North – Cushendall -where my father was a teacher. Our stay there was provisional - we were always on our way to somewhere else. My parents lived in all kinds of double binds – they were enlightened nationalists who admired the welfare state but had a Southerner's contempt for Northern Ireland. They came to despise the grubby failures of the South as well, but were uneasy with our childish – and unsuccessful - attempts to integrate in Cushendall.

Every summer we made the pilgrimage to our granny in Dublin. There were the party pieces to learn, the new dresses to make, the better versions of ourselves to present to our relations. Then the awful decisions about which dolls to take and which to abandon and how we would fit it all into one bag – let alone carry it.

Dublin made its appearance through the echoing chequered halls of Amiens Street station from which we staggered under our luggage into the unfamiliar taxi with the jump-seats which caused the ritual squabble. We crossed the smelly river - *Wouldn't you think they'd clean it up?* passed the streets and streets of buildings that appeared so tall. There was the sidelong romance of Roberts café where my parents had met, Leeson Park where a caterwauling cat had nearly fallen victim to my father's airgun, and the red brick lookalikes of Morehampton Road with their door covers flapping stripily. Finally there was our granny's house only distinguishable from its neighbours by its black gate. Why were urban houses so like biscuits? But we were suddenly awkward, subduing our Northern accents and pretending to understand the other children's games. After all, this was our real home. This summer life presented us with exotic choices – shoals of relations, outings to the Zoo with its elephant and pony rides, and the jangling tram to Howth. Even the chocolate was strange. Then there were the shops. For famished bookaholics like myself and my sister four bookshops within walking distance of Stephen's Green were heaven indeed. We weren't supposed to enter Hanna's as our father had been expelled for overbrowsing in his penniless student days and no child of his was to purchase their Enid Blyton or Patricia Lynch from such a mean-minded establishment. Books were horrendously expensive but a dedicated reader could gobble up a few chapters every visit before making the final decision.

In the shining halls of Switzer's and Brown Thomas you could squirt yourself with fancy perfume while the make-up lady's back was turned. In Jules we sat on twirly stools in front of majestic mirrors where my mother indulged one of her few extravagances – proper haircuts for us. Not that we always liked the results.

It was in Dublin that our parents sometimes lost the run of their ingrained frugality- they brought us into Joyce's clattery café – Bewley's - and even asked us what we wanted. I was bemused by such unaccustomed choice. Should I have the known and loved meringue or try the piebald swirly concoction which might be delightful or awful – but which you certainly couldn't leave on your plate?

Best of all there were the other Dubliners – the real ones with their flat accents, their quick put-downs, their funny snobberies, the fashionable rubbing shoulders with the sleazy. Everywhere slivers of conversation whetted my appetite for the fuller story. I was always half scared, half thrilled, missing the quietness and beauty of Cushendall, but yet – long before I had heard of Anna Livia - knowing that I wanted to jump into those urban streams and coast along them forever.

Collection for Gargantuan Hill
John O' Malley

Times heart beat is off again.
Mite boxes outside the bank,
Should wine bring more blasphemy?
I'll hope for some such thing,
As April without warning
Prepares old heart to sing.

Why not say good... goodbye?
Magnolia has no way to sigh.
Mechanical mood must wink its eye
Grant lunacy to-day to die.

July Morning In Moy, West Clare
Paddy Glavin

Bird calls
with fragrances
from bridal

wreaths of
honeysuckle and
meadow-sweet.

A skylight over
the Atlantic discovers
shy flowers.

A swallow
loops
into the byre.

Cows stand off
beyond
the rushes.

Stone walls
guard
unforgiving fields.

A swing
lies idle
on a Fir tree.

The Burren
John Haughton

Pine martens playing on
Craggy rocks of
Limestone's
Lunar Landscapes

Ravens soaring
O'er Mullaghmore's
Sister Mountains
Enclosing disappearing
Turloughs

Spring Gentian
Bloody Cranesbill
Bird's Foot Trefoil
Flora Fantasia

Preserve
Conserve
Protect
Unique
Treasure
Trove

Making A Cup Of Tea For Anne
Eddie Phillips

I return to the bedroom for diary and pencil,
I can squeeze something from the morning.

"Great mug!"(Drinker's compliment or brewer's title)
"Special brew for you Anne, fifteen second spoon."

Skill acclaim recalls spooning reflection:
In a staffroom an Ann's speech becomes intermittent

And breaks, "sorry, I'm watching you do the tea".
"Yes Ann, it makes our morning special".

Here I ponder what's special about the ordinary.
I make myself another and watch me.

I flush mug to pre-heat
I drop bag and finger it flat.

It surfs the surface, rapids of steam and bubbles.
Unmerciful aimed gush follows its floundering dodges.

Dead in the water, now torpedoed by spoon
Back to the depths.

Spoon handle gripped with chiselling firmness,
The essence released like poetry making wonderous the ordinary.

Back on the surface the whale plays with the visitor's portion:
Spoon back extracts a playful celebration.

That's the brewing, barrelling, bottling and pouring:
A lazy steam in sunlight is for your nosing.

Excavations
John Walsh

Shards of meaning
No longer fit together.
The burnished bowl has lost
The rim of its design.
Elsewhere the glint of gold
Gladdens and then disappoints
With its base retort.
We tip the spoil of life
To let it subside.
The layers interleave,
Ash and clay conceal.
Life leaves its postholes
For others to read.

The Holiday
Sue Brown

Usually the route has no focus.
As I go home, the old man watches
as the daises disturb his lawn,
the boys playing disturb the letter
I am thinking and the aches of
weary arms and heart disrupt
the landscape I walk in.

But today only the old ladies
left to sun, with the caring young,
figure in the tumult of green.
Green-ruffle trees, green taffeta
lawns, half unmowed and the mowers gone —
I might be tiptoeing through a painting,
pausing to decide on the shadows of sky.

White Gloves
Máiride Woods

White gloves and deportment go together – they belong to a
world that's vanished and they have vanished – almost. I've
always loathed white gloves and for years my life was free of
them. But when my daughter was in the home stretch for her
First Communion she started drooling over frilly finger coverings.
"There is no theological reason for white gloves," I declared but
she wasn't impressed.
"I'll pay for them out of my Communion money," she countered.
"Over my dead body," I said. Communion money is also theolog-
ically suspect She smiled at me pityingly.

I don't like separable garments; they always get separated
from me. And aeons ago when I was a schoolgirl the state of
one's gloves was presumed to reflect the state of one's soul – and
mine gave cause for concern. My gloves were either absent, single or soiled.

White gloves are for decorative waiting; you wear them to
make a good impression. At our school we did a lot of waiting.
Instead of having oil ready beside our lamps like the Wise Virgins
in the Bible, we were expected to have a perfect uniform complete with spotless gloves always to hand. Then if one was suddenly called to present a bouquet to a visiting dignitary, all would
be well – flesh would not touch flesh, the white glove would inter-
vene. The ungloved had to skulk at the back of the ceremonial
line keeping their hands hidden. Pockets, needless to remark,
were only for handkerchiefs.

In Little Women I found a kindred spirit. Jo March, Louisa
Alcott's alter ego had all my problems with gloves and other items
of female attire. And she realised what a tremendous waste of
time all these dress conventions are. Not quite as bad as Chinese

foot binding but stifling nevertheless. Yet Jo wanted to be popular, fashionable, loved – and the state of one's gloves seemed crucial to this quest. Jo did have one advantage over me; she had Meg, an elder sister who was able to share her pair of decent gloves when a formal party threatened. At school I felt the loneliness of my gloveless state. My mother – a woman of sense – did not understand the need for pristine whiteness in gloves.

"Won't these do?" she would say, holding up an odd set one of which bore the marks of a close encounter with some ink. "No one will notice," she added but the nuns always did. Although I knew she had the right attitude, in the Child of Mary line I longed for the dreary sparkle of regulation white. *Tout passe* however, as our French teacher used to say and I left school and tried to catch up with my laid-back generation in UCD. My sole surviving white glove sank to the bottom of my drawer under the weight of beads and sarongs. For three years it was jeans and smocks and the odd dress. Then graduation day dawned and I strolled into the Great Hall. Consternation! The other girls were wearing –every one of them- white gloves. How had this happened, I fumed, scrunching up my less than perfect hands? Why had nobody told me? Where had all those relics of Convent decency been lurking? I scowled at the suddenly demure girl graduates. I would shake the President's hand flesh to flesh, the way the men did. And yet if some fairy godmother had slipped me passable white gloves that morning, I'm sure I would have given in and worn them. Just like I gave in to my daughter. She had her white gloves and I never saw a penny of the Communion money!

White gloves were closely related to deportment- a word that goes with etiquette, regulation lengths for shorts, and those hate ful sylphs who could glide around with several books on their heads. It was the bane of ugly duckling girls' lives for grace was needed to achieve deportment and this was something I lacked.

My school had a system of merit, order and deportment marks which penalised breaches of rules. In those days the need for a constant drip feed of praise was unknown; in our teachers' eyes the main danger was pride coming before a fall; and they worked to prevent this. Deportment marks were reserved for trivial offences: - the unseemly consumption of food or the absence of a beret. It was a matter of honour to be hatless outside the school grounds but the nuns fought a rearguard action armed with deportment marks.

The word deportment brings back most vividly the misery of being physically awkward. I was the sort of child whose feet were irresistibly drawn to dog-turds, whose knees were always bloody or scabby, whose very approach caused ink-wells to fly. The unresolved puzzle of left and right had made dancing class a torture. As for team games, I was always the last to be picked – and with reason. My problems were compounded by an early growth spurt which left me head and shoulders over my nimble schoolmates. "How tall you've got," people would chorus, as I shrank into the furniture, feeling like Alice after she'd made the wrong choice of medicine. My parents worried about my appearance; my feet turned in, my shoulders were round, my back crooked. "Stand up straight," came the call a dozen times a day. One summer they took me to buy built-up shoes the ultimate humiliation for an eleven year old. There's a shoe-shop in Dublin that narrowly escaped arson.

By the time I went away to boarding school, I felt like the Hunchback of Notre Dame. Being the youngest in my class didn't help; the role of youngest is only suited to those with Shirley Temple curls and a touch of the gambolling lamb. When my school wanted a mascot they picked someone else. I was the wrong size and my deportment was deplorable.

It was deplorable enough to draw the attention of the head nun who arranged after-school deportment classes for me. Oh the ignominy! The first day I arrived in the staff room, stiff with rage and humiliation to find that the young PT teacher was equally fed-up.

"I haven't volunteered for this any more than you have," she said. "We'll just sit and talk – but if you hear the wolf coming, lie down on the floor and move your legs up and down."

So for several Fridays we sat in the staff room gossiping our ears pealed for the rattle of beads.

"You'll be fine in a couple of years," she reassured me. I didn't care what I was like as long as people left me alone. Forty years later I remember her kindness and the kindness of an uncle who told my parents to stop fussing, that when I was old enough for fellows I'd be grand.

Gradually all those dainty sylphs and Shirley Temples caught up with me. Some of them passed me out in the bosom stakes but I wasn't jealous. Inkwells gave way to biros; my turd avoidance skills improved; and my parents switched their worrying to the Cuban missile crisis. There were still things I cried off for fear of exhibiting my awkwardness – I never learned to jive for instance – But mostly I passed as normal.

By then deportment was on the way out. Maeve Binchy lambasted it on the Late Late Show; nuns started wearing casual clothes. And around me a great silence started falling. The "Stand up Straights" died away. It wasn't that I'd turned into a swan. But the major advantage of adult life is that people don't feel morally bound to improve you. By the time you're middle-aged you can be as crooked as you like. No one cares!

May We Be...
John O' Malley

We are gathered in the nets of God

Happy go lucky symbol of fish!
Local fishermen bring Howth mackerel
Up to me where I work.

Invariably they fail to clean and gut.
Grill them on the spot I say
Or give them away again.

A child comes at night, in exchange
For blank tickets promises a big one.
They ate it themselves for supper.

Smell off my hands, hair, clothes,
Every ticket I touch.
Customers wonder where it comes from.

Kippers coming out my eyes and ears.
Feel almost part of the sea
Gastronomically speaking I guess.

Blighter's Rock
Eddie Phillips

Never admit drying up,
Call it a visit to Blighter's Rock.
And don't try a re-float
At the watering hole,
Like a friend of mine.
He turned Limericks and Haikus
On the barman.
But he shipped some shock with a single line.
"You're Bard Mr. Puny-verse."

My dog Ming
John Haughton

My dog Ming
For a walk I bring
Brown and rare
He's like a bear
Looks fierce and strong
Like a mighty gong
From the land of Tao
He is a Chow

Migrating
John Walsh

I was born inland;
As far from the sea as possible
Under the Ballyhoura Hills.
Our school room window
Was filled with its own lesson
In Old Red Sandstone;
Lying from east to west
Like a stranded whale,
Except when hidden by the rain.
I , who craved the sun, moved
Northwards to settle
Where Middle Stone Age people
Had squatted on their midden
Of shells and bones by the sea
Which sucked and sipped at their heels
On this low shore.
Watched over by Red Rock.

Badminton Capers
Paddy Glavin

Wham! - Have you ever heard the sound of a shuttlecock collid-
ing with taut strings? The first time I saw a game of badminton
was in Bayside community hall when I joined a newly formed
club. I watched the intricate patterns and parabolas of a shuttlecock's flight over a sixteen by seven metres badminton court.
What hidden design of beauty lay behind this game? Was it the
allurement of the white on white clad female figures that guarded the net at the front in the mixed doubles? Perhaps it was a mixture of ballet and fencing with players using rackets instead of
swords that fascinated me?

I did not realize then, the changes this sport would bring to
my life, and to the lives of my fellow club members. New friendships were made in a relatively relaxed atmosphere. We learned
new skills. It was vital to use the wrist when serving, and in the
slow movement of a drop shot. When I first gripped the three and
a half-ounce racket I watched the flight of the shuttlecock from
opponents as I positioned myself underneath its vertical drop. I
blinked and the feathered missile landed on my head. The other
players laughed, but with practice I avoided 'fresh airs', and any-
how miss- hitting enhanced the hilarity. My life was transformed
from being a middle-aged couch potato to becoming an active
player in a newly discovered sport.

A year went by and the club enrolled in competitions. Ten
teams were selected from the hundred or so members. We were
now in the Leinster League. The club became competitive with
people vying for places on teams. This meant playing matches
anywhere between Bettystown county Meath and Wicklow town,
and inland to the boundary of the Pale.

Late one night before Christmas in a ramshackle barn in Clane I mopped a wet floor before beginning play. By midnight I was mopping my brow exhausted after a match. We lost, but the bar was still open and our hosts gave us a fine supper including helpings of plum pudding. However the hospitality did not lessen the pain of defeat.

Before Christmas the annual club tournament took place. The adrenalin flowed as if we were in a medieval joust or a trial by combat. On this occasion the competitors wore 'Fancy Dress'. My costume was a remote image of "Boy George". With the ingredient of humour I relaxed and won first prize: a voucher for a turkey. We consumed the bird for Christmas dinner, so the mantelpiece is bereft of any trophies except for my other half's games in a competition a miniature obelisk, which she acquired as a prize for not winning any matches!

In the New Year the club employed a coach of international repute. When we were unable to keep up with her demands or execute strokes correctly, she tortured us with 'press ups'. I recall seeing innumerable bodies of middle years stretched on the floor. She shouted on the court
"Kill it". In striving to obey we were almost killing ourselves! Competitive badminton demanded a fencer's speed of reflex, and a gymnast's agility. Playing for the club was a source of pride in the parish. Patrick Kavanagh's poem Epic captures the feeling.
"Which was more important? I inclined
to lose my faith in Ballyrush and Goirtin
Till Homer's ghost came whispering to my mind
He said: I made the Iliad from such
A local row. Gods make their own importance".

The poem reminds me how badminton became a fundamental part of our lives in the parish of Bayside until time caught up with us. As we became older winning matches was more difficult and the physical demands beckoned the now silver-haired members to retire. The senior club closed eventually but thankfully the young people are still playing.

In these days of professional sport, I reflect on those badminton times and the feelings of camaraderie created with people of all ages within and outside the community. The regular exercise improved our health and we had no obesity problems. I know that playing the game was an ideal recreation in a parish and if football is a game for all, badminton is a game for all ages!

Urban Curlews
Máiride Woods

After the traffic slackens
I hear the curlews calling...
Even when I'm on the Internet
Their cry lodges in my brain
Speaking of loss and death
And the raw wind
Before dawn.

They call softly, persistently,
Through marshy-syllabled words,
Through arguments and advertisements.
They conjure up black wrecks
On stretches of unpopulated water
And the raw wind
Of sorrow.

My Dad the Rabbi
Sue Brown

"Try to forgive...', he said. Try to understand
how afraid hard people are. They live in a fear
we do not know because the God of our people
is like a pillar of flame. Try to walk in their shoes
and feel what fear can do.' Anguish filled his
sensitive mind, but he was not afraid.
He would take anyone back, like a long-lost child
or even a brother with his own eyes lit by anguish
of a story hard to tell. 'you cannot live unless
you are loving people. Take them all as your family
always to have the front door swing open
and the hall light lit. Always forgive.'
Oh Dad, so soon to die so young,
with every ounce of my body and mind
I try....In it I come close to you
unexpectedly. I see you stand near
your eyes clear, and interested
in my life, hopeful even.
'It's always worth trying, even if
you lose. Love all you can,
break the rules of expected social
behaviour to share life; be punished for it
but not by me. I will be beside you
and working for it,' you say
almost eagerl, 'so you lose.
You are alive inside.'
'I cannot help trying,' I say
hanging my head at the worldly
foolishness. 'I know,' you say,
'we are a family. I am your father.
I understand.'

'Is it worth the pain and confusing battles
with loved people to reach and love more?
To love after being told to go away, or worse?'
'Worth it? Yes, of course. It is the only way.
Now let's get on with it,' he says. 'We'll plan...
I need you all to forgive...'
'Love wins, Dad,' I cry with tears of joy,
exasperation,deep sorrow,
love awake to your call, and you so here with me,
and with us all. Thanks for helping me in
my life's loves. Adult to adult, father to
daughter he looks at me; he is my friend,
my family's bonding teacher – how, I don't
know, but he never died at all.

The Shannon on a warm sunny evening.
John O' Malley

I look not as a stranger on your waves,
The rapture you create, teacher great.

Oh past personality, where comes our wage,
Thirsters for song, just sedate.

Words mentioned loosely apart
Whatever admission, we work for art.

Controller of souls, luxuriously in charge
Us passing by, you own the barge.

Break waves on an empty shore
Show the power of make believe
No longer are our hearts in love
At this time we bring a sieve.
Our rocking horse an hour ago
Was pictured when the sun was right.
 Before we are solaced more
We languish in that light.
And then musty dust is neat
Positively ignored at our feet.
No dancing at all this night
What evidence we have, will suffice.

The Push And Resist
Eddie Phillips

You wouldn't come with me
In to the poetry mode
And watch ourselves
Through the poets' eyes
With little fingers linked.

No. You, like a Mona Lisa:
Face to my left, with your gaze
Quizzical in the distance
Out past my right;
And your mind, an oar
At full stroke in my waters.

And yes. Me standing, arms crossed,
Fists in my armpits.

23 April 2004

Night Work
Sue Brown

Today I saw the evening star
in the twilight of my life.
Old loves like houses, solid, plain
mark the pale wide road of stone
with places been, and flow of sun.

And now to tools I come back
in the shadowy shed, to a wooden table
wood-creaky, with the leather
last-worked waiting; here my life is
like a wound and like a love.

My lamp sheds light, and outside
A small answering star begins to bloom,
small furrow-light in a field of time,
sprouting among soft billows of blue.

Transitions
John Walsh

Where the land meets the mud and mud meets the sea
Where solid runs to ooze and then to a fluid.
This is the place where the eye follows the soul
Down to the deep wells of knowing.

Where the glance meets the eye and eye meets a smile.
Where a nod leads to a gasp and then to a touch.
This is the place where a kiss takes the breath
Down to the deep wells of knowing.

Where body meets the skin and skin meets the soul
Where the the flesh and blood brings heat to the bone.
This is the place where pleasure flays pain
Down to the deep wells of knowing.

Where the mind meets the light and light brings the day.
Where the beat of the sun exceeds the joy of the night.
This is the place where the black doubts appear
And drown the deep wells of knowing.

Self Defeat
John O' Malley

There I was well on in my career working on a presentation with Stubbs Gazette, me father of six here with an accountant from Torquay road, Foxrock. What I was really doing out there was trying to get liquidation accounts for debt collection, that's the way I worked with Dun & Bradstreet. I saw every accountant who would meet me. But this one turned out differently. I realised I knew this man – a smile from him, Andy Butler yes? Captain Rockwell College 1959. He kicked a penalty from the touchline and held Crescent to a draw at Thomond Park, Limerick in the last few minutes. We lost the replay at Musgrave Park, Cork, 9-0, the following week.

One of our players at the time who was young enough was heard to say, "there's always next year." Alas! but not for most of us, I mused on my way home in the company car that day. How my life might have been so different. It's amazing how the pain had eased, but then at seventeen years of age my world had crumbled.

They used to say a misspent youth meant snooker halls and cigarettes. Our family were not allowed to hang around, but rugby and other games we played and practiced to our hearts content. My downfall though was with the oval ball. In a male dominated society, it made you think you were somebody – the peer group looked up to you, might even buy you a drink – later great for shifting girls at the dances just because you played. After thirty years, that day in the eighties was the first time I had rolled the nightmare over for quite some time.

Crescent were on a roll that year of 59, we won the Bowen shield, scored over eighty points but it was not to be our year. Even those medals got lost, I guess by the coach and trainer Jesuit

Father Gerry Guinane, World War 1 veteran and Chaplain. I sure was on the right side of him, played hard, and got a try against Rockwell before Christmas. We were just too complacent.

Father Lehane Holy Ghost Father plotted our downfall all that spring. Rockwell College in their blue and white hoops were not the elite team for nothing, all they had to do was knock us out of our stride. Once the game plan was upset we lost our rhythm. I can still see them coming through the lineout. They tore at our back line, wheeled our scrums but they killed us with their tackling. We were pale scarecrows run off our feet. The silence in the dressing room was palpable and of course at school the next day.

Was I a callow youth? Naive, innocent or just plain stupid. Father Guinane diplomat, Munster selector, was also my maths teacher. I handed up an empty copybook for many years. You could buy the entrance fee to college then for a fiver with five passes including Irish and English. Surprise surprise! I didn't do too well in his subject.

What might have been? Even then we lived for our privileges. In theory you could get into the Irish army if you got a Munster schools cap. A nod was as good as a wink with the Ginner. Win the Munster schools cup and who knows with me in the F.C.A (Foras Cosunta Aitiul) Lieutenant John O' Malley in the regular army was on the cards. But it wasn't to be. That place kicker, now Mr Butler F.C.A (Fellow of the Charted Accountants) healed my old wounds. However I did get the Munster jersey for my sixtieth birthday. I may write the bluffers guide to rugby football if I ever get over that senior schools cup final defeat.

Bishop Casey by John Haughton written in Galway City on the banks of the Corrib River

A cloud hangs over Galway
Bishop Casey has gone
The Pastor went astray
His flock left to pray

Loud Corrib waters roar
Hushed whispers soar
Round cathedral proud
Clothed in lonely shroud

A body blow
For seeds he sowed
The Holy See
Did so decree
For sins of flesh
No friendly crèche
The 'lost sheep'
In exile bleats.

Felled Without Trial

Thomas Delaney

The sycamore cried and then it died
Fingal council was unaware of its tears
It was twenty metres high a beautiful hide.
Some residents said that they were in the way for years.

The council intimated it was cheaper to chop them down to the
Ground
The felling is so telling, it reeks of clandestine sneaks.
There are too many trees they say, why the frown
They said their decision was not taken lightly, tongues in cheeks

The council barks, it is their protective coat
To that tree it is a skin of total beauty
They said that they were sad to see them go, how remote
Forest friends, were maddened towards a sense of duty

Uprooted by a scandalous foul, of jack booting
We the council will do as we please, to those trees
We will move from street to street in arrogant uprooting
We are indifferent to all those irritant residential pleas.

Spring
John Haughton

Warm breezes blowing
Lawn mowers mowing
Season of luscious growth

Meadow-grass dancing
A thousand stallions prancing
Majestic Mother Nature

Wood pigeons cooing
Milch cows mooing
Cups overflowing

Fields of corn
Fields of barley
Promise to ripen early

Fields of rape
Vines and grape
Days never-ending

Farmer's perspiration
Artist's inspiration
Rain's precipitation

Who made the sky?
Baby sheep to cry?
The Great Unknown!

In Dreams the world is the nest of mankind
Paddy Glavin

A robin darts,
scans the earth
on the lookout
for a meal.

A sparrow clinging
on the nut basket:
the soul of generosity
as robin pecks the fallout.

Dun of orange and grey
darts back to its sanctuary,
a shrub with prayers
ever in leaf.

One day a sparrow
dallies at the bird-table,
the stealth flying hawk
swoops and clasps its prey.

Robin hides
keeps a vigilant
and bright eye out
for collateral damage.

Now the sky fills
with birds from everywhere.
Flamingoes, and Galapagos finches
and from China one winged peehees

fly in couples.
Like a thunderbolt
the eagle swoops
and silences the chorus.

Biographies

Eddie Phillips winged his way from West Wicklow in the early 60s. (He says, 'thank you Dublin for having me.') He found Anne, a Dublin girl, and they've nested in Bayside for nearly thirty years. Always a word fan Eddie, it took the Trinity Writers' Group of Donaghmede Library to get him going with the quill. Along with the attendant reading that goes with writing he feels he's only in the early foothills of a Rockies adventure.

Frances Glavin was born in North Kilkenny. She wrote in secondary school and was a member of Klear in the eighties. Frances participated in workshops run by Mairide Woods and Noel McLoughlin. Her work appeared in two Klear publications, and in Trinity's last two books: The Jericho Road and Concetti 2000.

John Haughton is author of, '*The Silver Lining*', which is the story of Lady Heath and the history of Irish aviation in the 1930s. He was editor of two anthologies of poems about the environment, written by pupils of the Ballyfermot schools, under the title, '*The Forest of Children Dreaming*'. This formed part of '*The Ballyfermot Schools Forest Project*' an innovative environmental project. John was co-editor of the Forest Friends Ireland/Cáirde na Coille anthology of poetry, '*Seeing the Wood and the Trees*'. Some of his poems are included in the Trinity Writer Group's publication, '*Trinity Collage*'.

After a typical childhood in East Limerick and North Tipperary
John O' Malley emerged to Liverpool Beatlemania, the buses and London factories in 1960-61. Then back to Dublin and U.C.D. Exposure to the arts and friendships made me develop my love for poetry. In 1970 I fell in love with June whom I married. I settled in Bayside and have lived and worked here ever since, helping to raise six children also. Through scouting and other parish work I met some wonderful people and a few writers like myself. I have published some of my work in various magazines over the years.

John Walsh was born in Kilmallock , Co. Limerick and grew up watching small towns die while horses were replaced by tractors. Early influences were The Limerick Leader and the BBC on longwave. Being close to life and nature and death provided the stimulus for early writings. Urban angst has added to that inspiration. Current obsessions include the transitions between water and land, sound and silence and growth and decay. He has been seeking asylum in the public service for the last thirty years.

Mairide Woods was born in Dublin but spent her childhood in Cushendall, Co Antrim. She writes poetry, short stories and radio drama. She won a Hennessy Award in 1992 and several awards for RTE. Her work has appeared in many Irish Anthologies. In her other life she has worked as a teacher and researcher. She has lived with her family in Bayside for almost thirty years.

Paddy Glavin was born and reared in Listowel and came to Dublin in the mid-fifties. While on the buses he joined a study group from where he went on to third level education. He became a teacher in 1970. He married Frances and they settled in Bayside in 1974. After retiring he took up writing poems and stories. In 1999 he won first prize in a Listowel Writers' Week Originals competition. He has contributed poems and stories to local and national anthologies.

Pat Boran is the author of four collections of poetry, short fiction for adults and children, and four non-fiction works including the popular writers' handbook: The Portable Creative Writing Workshop.
He is Programme Director of the annual Dublin Writers Festival.

Sue Brown grew up in a rural New England town. Her father was from a Lithuanian refugee family and many Polish refugees had bought small farms in the Connecticut River valley. She came to Ireland as a student, fell in love, married and moved to Bayside. Here her son and daughter grew up and one of the aspects of Bayside she loves most is the natural and nurturing setting it provides for children. She trains primary school teachers in storytelling, sharing books with children, and creating puppets.

Paula Meehan was born in Dublin where she still lives. The poems here are set on Burrow Beach where she walks regularly with her black dog. The beach itself, and the esturial land at Baldoyle, give her a perspective on eternity, and never fail to counter the daily fret.

"I personally don't have categories like professional or otherwise – the blank page is a great leveller and the muse is just as likely (more likely in my experience) to strike the beginner as the old hand. Maybe the old hand has learned a few wily moves to make the most of the visitation"

Thomas Delaney has published a book of poems entitled *"The Poet Asks Why"*. He is a prolific poet and teaches Appreciation of Literature and Creative Writing in Greendale Community College.

Theo Dorgan is a poet, broadcaster and scriptwriter. His libretto *Jason and The Argonauts*, with music by Howard Goodall, was premiered this summer in the Royal Albert Hall, London. His latest book is *Sailing for home*, published by Penguin Ireland in October.